The Girls' Book of Friendship

of

How to be the

Best Friend Ever

Written by Gemma Reece
Illustrated by Katy Jackson
Edited by Sally Pilkington
Designed by Zoe Quayle

The Girls' Book of Friendship

of

HOW TO BE THE BEST FRIEND EVER

SCHOLASTIC INC.

New York   Toronto   London   Auckland
Sydney   Mexico City   New Delhi   Hong Kong

Library of Congress Cataloging-in-Publication data is available.

ISBN 978-0-545-22327-0

First published in Great Britain in 2010 by Buster Books, an imprint of Michael O'Mara Books
Limited, 9 Lion Yard, Tremadoc Road, London SW4 7NQ
www.mombooks.com/busterbooks

Cover design by Angie Allison
(from an original design by www.blacksheep-uk.com)

12 11 10 9 8 7 6 5 4 3 2 1   10 11 12 13 14 15/0

Printed in the U.S.A.
First American edition, May 2010

23

NOTE TO READERS

CONTENTS

How to make a
    friendship locket   8

How to help a
    friend in need   10

Friendship games   11

How to make a
    friendship survival kit   13

How to show the world
    you're friends   15

How to make a
    friendship coat of arms   17

What kind of friend
    are you?   19

How to make a
    four-way friends' pizza   23

The golden rules
    of friendship   25

How to make a
    group T-shirt   27

How to be friends
    with a vampire   30

How to make
    friendship cookies   32

Why everybody needs
    good friends   34

How to make a
    friendship flower   36

How to use
    "the power of pals"   38

How to make a superfast
    friendship bracelet   40

Imaginary-friend fun   42

How to make
    a friendship box   43

How to have the
    ultimate sleepover   46

When is a friend
    not a true friend?   48

You know you spend too much
    time together when . . .   51

How to make a
    friendship fortune-teller   53

Five reasons why pets
    make great friends   57

Real friends or fake friends?   58

How to seal your friendship   59

How to make a
    personalized birthday card   62

How to "go fish" for friends   65

How to draw a
    silhouette of your friend   69

How to hold a
    friendship award ceremony   71

The friendship doctor   74

How to make a clubhouse   77

How to make
    floor cushions   78

How to make up after
    an argument   81

How to make a friendship
    time capsule   82

How to make friends
  with yourself   85

How to make friends
  with a celebrity   86

How to give a
  mad-cap makeover   88

How to create your own
  "friendspeak"   91

The dos and don'ts
  of safe friendships   93

Reasons why boys
  make good friends, too   94

How to tell if one of your
  friends is a werewolf   96

How to play "the
  winning smile"   98

How to forgive your friend   100

Daring deeds for
  best friends to do   102

How to make new friends   104

How to write a letter to your
  pen pal   106

Three instant boredom busters
  for you and your friends   109

How to start a girl band   111

How to stay friends for life   114

How to make friends
  with your parents   116

How to hold a swap meet   117

HOW TO MAKE A FRIENDSHIP LOCKET

A friendship locket is a pendant, worn around the neck, that opens to reveal pictures of your best friends. Wearing one helps you keep your friends close to you, even when you are apart.

You will need:

- 20 inches of ribbon • a small metal hinge 1 1/4 x 3/4 inches (from a crafts store) • a sheet of pretty gift wrap • a pencil • scissors • glue • 2 small photos of your friends

1. Take your length of ribbon and thread it through one of the holes at the top of the hinge.

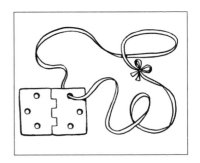

2. Turn your piece of gift wrap over, so that it is pattern-side down. Place the open hinge on top and draw around it. Cut this out so you are left with a rectangle. Cut this rectangle in half, widthwise, so that you have two small rectangles.

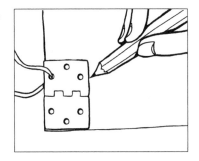

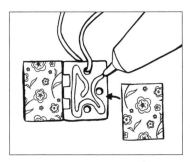

3. Apply a thin layer of glue to each half of your hinge and stick each rectangle on it, positioning it by sliding it around while the glue is still wet. Be careful not to position them too close together, so that the hinge opens easily. Leave this to dry.

4. When your hinge is dry, take one of your photos and position the closed hinge over the part you want to appear in your locket. Draw around the hinge and then cut the shape out. Repeat this with your other photo.

5. Place your hinge so that it is pattern-side down and carefully apply a thin layer of glue to the inside surfaces. Take one of your photos very carefully by the edges and stick it on the hinge so that the head points toward the ribbon. Repeat for the other photo and then leave your locket open to dry.

6. Once the glue is dry, close the locket and wear it around your neck.

HOW TO HELP
A FRIEND IN NEED

One of the most important things friends do is help each other out when one of them is going through a tough time. Follow these dos and don'ts to make sure that you are being a good friend when your best bud is feeling blue.

DO "be there" for your friend. This means finding the time to be with her when she needs support, even if you are busy. If she is very sad, you might want to try to rearrange your plans so that you can spend extra time with her.

DO show your friend you care. Call her when you are not together, or send her a little card to let her know that she is not alone and that you are thinking of her.

DO offer advice. If your friend comes to you with a problem, try to help her find a solution. If her problem seems very serious, encourage her to turn to an adult you both trust to help her figure out what to do.

DON'T be upset with your friend if she doesn't take your advice and decides to do her own thing. It's her life, after all.

DON'T go on and on about a time when something similar happened to you. This is your friend's problem, so give her the space to talk it out.

DO stock up on cookies and tissues. Let your friend have a good cry on your shoulder, and share some cookies with her (see page 32). Soon she'll be well on the way to feeling fine again.

FRIENDSHIP GAMES

Is one of your friends always the leader? Learn to share your roles with these fun games. They aren't about winning or losing – you all need to work together, or it's game over!

WE ALL STAND TOGETHER

This game helps you and your friend learn to work together.

Stand back-to-back with your friend, with your shoulders touching hers, then lock your arms together with hers at the elbows.

Now, very slowly, try to sit down on the floor without unlocking your arms. This is much more difficult than it sounds.

Once you have managed to sit down, don't unlink your arms. Instead, try to stand up again. This is even more difficult and can leave you in some very funny positions.

True-friend tip. Make this game even more fun by asking another friend to join you as you try sitting down and standing up again, locked together as three. Keep on adding people until all of your friends are in the circle!

COPYCATS

In any group of good pals, each friend should get her chance to take the lead. You will need at least four friends to play this game.

Form a circle with your friends and ask one of them to leave the room for a few minutes. She will be the Guesser. The rest of you have to decide who is going to be the Leader, making everyone left a Copycat.

Invite the Guesser back into the room and allow her to rejoin the circle. The Leader and the Copycats must now start swinging their arms backward and forward.

While you are all swinging your arms, the Leader must also make other small movements, such as sticking out her tongue or tapping her foot. The Copycats must copy these movements as soon as they see them without making it at all obvious who it is they are copying. The Guesser must watch very closely and try to figure out who the Leader is.

When the Guesser has managed to identify the Leader, it is the Leader's turn to become the Guesser so that the game can start again.

True-friend tip. To make the game super-challenging, the Leader should discuss which movements she is going to use with the Copycats before the Guesser comes back into the room. That way the Copycats will know what to look out for and will be able to copy her right away.

HOW TO MAKE A FRIENDSHIP SURVIVAL KIT

This pretty pouch of trinkets is simple to make and is the ideal gift for someone close to your heart. It will remind you and your pals how to stay friends forever.

You will need:

- a large clean handkerchief • a cotton ball
- a piece of gold thread or gift ribbon
- a small candle • a button • a Band-Aid
- a pebble • a small roll of tape
- a piece of writing paper • a pen

1. Lay the handkerchief out in front of you and place all the items in the middle of it, except for the gold thread, the paper, and the pen.

2. Take the piece of paper and, in your best handwriting, write out the friendship survival kit's user guide on the next page.

THIS FRIENDSHIP SURVIVAL KIT CONTAINS:

- A golden thread, because friendship is the golden thread that ties our lives together

- A cotton ball, to cushion any rocky roads ahead

- A candle, because you are a shining light

- A Band-Aid, for healing hurt feelings

- A handkerchief, for drying tears

- A pebble, because you are my rock

- Some tape, because good friends stick together

- A button, because if you can't say anything nice, button your mouth!

3. Fold your survival kit's user guide in half several times until it is as small as you can make it, then put it in the center of your handkerchief with the other items.

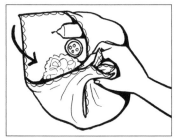

4. Gather the corners of your handkerchief together to form a pouch.

5. Tie your gold thread or gift ribbon around the top in a pretty bow to keep your items inside.

6. Give your survival kit to a good friend to let her know you will be her BFF – Best Friend Forever.

HOW TO SHOW THE WORLD YOU'RE FRIENDS

Okay, so you know who your friends are — now it's time to let others in on the secret. Follow these great tips to show the world who your favorite people are.

CREATE A "BEST-FRIEND" HANDSHAKE

When you meet up with your friends, performing your own personal handshake is the perfect way to prove you are best buds. A best-friend handshake needs to be loud and bold so that other people can see and hear it. You can either make up your own or use the one below.

1. Stand opposite your friend and gently bump your right fist against hers.

2. Do the same with the left fist.

3. Clap your right hands together and slowly slide them backward and apart.

4. End with a big backslapping hug.

GET THE LOOK OF FRIENDSHIP

Wearing exactly the same clothes as your friend can look over the top and is a definite fashion no-no. Coordinating your look, however, can be totally cool. For example, if one of you wears black jeans and a white top, the other could wear white jeans and a black top. This can look seriously stylish and will get you lots of attention.

BE BUDDIES, BRIGHT AND BEAUTIFUL

Choose a color that you both like and try to each wear an item in that color every day. You can keep it simple – for example, add a purple hair band or wear a lilac camisole under your shirt – or you can go wild with your chosen shade. Do whatever you want to show that you are friends!

MAKE A NAME FOR YOURSELF

Really close friends never call each other by their real names, but use nicknames instead. To come up with nicknames for yourself and your friends, make up silly words based on your real names, such as Lyndependent for Lynn, or Madster for Madison. Alternatively, use nicknames that have to do with your personalities – for example, if one of your friends is always laughing, she could be called The Giggler. Don't be afraid to mix things up a bit – a friend who is very tall could be called Shorty, or a friend with very dark hair could be called Blondie.

True-friend tip. Make sure you agree on your names together. Calling someone a name that she doesn't like or agree to is not friendly or okay. It could hurt her feelings and even get you into some serious trouble.

HOW TO MAKE A FRIENDSHIP COAT OF ARMS

A coat of arms is a shield made up of pictures that represent the person who owns the shield. In medieval times, they were used by knights to identify themselves on the battlefield. Make your own to symbolize your group of friends.

You will need:

• a pencil • felt-tip pens • a sheet of 11 x 17-inch paper or poster board • a ruler • scissors • a photograph of you and your friends • a glue stick • old magazines • a picture of where you all live

1. Using your pencil, draw this shield shape on your paper as large as you can, and cut it out.

2. Use a ruler to draw a horizontal line dividing the shield in half, as shown. Then divide the top half of your shield in half.

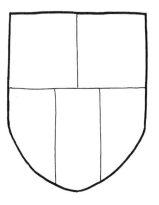

3. Divide the bottom portion of your shield into three as shown. Your shield should now be divided into five sections.

4. Glue the photo of you and your friends in the top left-hand section of your shield.

5. Together with your friends, go through your old magazines and look for a picture of the thing you all love best. For instance, if you can't get enough of eating delicious ice cream, try to find a really cool picture of a sundae, or if you all really love dolphins, find a picture of one and cut it out. If you can't find a picture, don't worry. Simply draw a dolphin on a fresh sheet of paper and cut it out. Stick this in the top right-hand section of your shield.

6. In the bottom left-hand section, put a picture of where you all live. You could find a postcard of your town or city to stick on, or you could take a photograph of a popular landmark.

7. In the bottom right-hand section, put a picture to represent someone you all admire and look up to. If this person is famous, look for a picture in your magazines and cut it out, or if it is someone you know, use a photograph.

8. Now you should think of a motto for your group of friends. A motto is a phrase that sums up the things you all think are most important. For example, "Laugh loud. Laugh a lot."

True-friend tip. Your coat of arms is very precious, as it is a symbol of your friendship. Take turns looking after it, and make sure you keep it safe.

WHAT KIND OF FRIEND ARE YOU?

Ask yourself the following questions and write down your answers on a piece of paper. The results will reveal how you fit into your group of friends.

1. Your friend asks your opinion of a new shirt that she was given as a present, because she doesn't love it. You think that the colors really clash. Do you . . .

> **A.** . . . . say that you think it might be a little over the top and that she could try to exchange it — but add that she looks good in anything?

> **B.** . . . . laugh and tell her you wouldn't be seen dead in it and neither should she?

> **C.** . . . . suggest that she keeps it and wears it, and starts a new trend? If she won't, you will!

2. It's a hot summer day and you see some friends having a water fight in the park, but you are supposed to be going home to do your chores. Do you . . .

> **A.** . . . wave, and arrange to meet them later, after you have been home and completed your tasks?

> **B.** . . . run to the store and buy some water balloons, then run back to the group and attack?

> **C.** . . . continue on your way? You'll have some lemonade to cool off while you're doing your chores.

3. At school, a friend gives you a note telling you she's been feeling down in the dumps. Do you . . .

> **A.** . . . arrange to meet her at lunchtime with all your other pals, so you can give her a hug and work out her problem?

> **B.** . . . give her a hug, make a weird face, and mess your hair up to make her laugh?

> **C.** . . . write a note back and ask what's wrong?

4. Your birthday is coming up. Do you . . .

> **A.** . . . wait until the day, then take slices of your birthday cake into school to share with everyone?

> **B.** . . . make sure everyone knows what day it is and invite your whole class to your party?

> **C.** . . . ask your parents to take you and your best friend on a trip to the local water park?

5. Two of your friends have had an argument. Do you . . .

A. . . . talk to them separately, tell them how important it is to you that you are all friends, and try to encourage them to see one another's point of view?

B. . . . immediately ditch them in favor of some new friends who seem to be more fun?

C. . . . leave them alone? It's better not to get involved. They'll get over it in time, as they always do!

6. Your friend confides in you that she has a huge crush on a boy in your class at school. Do you . . .

A. . . . share *your* secret crush with her and spend hours together coming up with ways that you can "accidentally bump into" the boys on the way home from school?

B. . . . immediately start talking to the boy and his friends so you can become better friends with him and set him up with your friend?

C. . . . do nothing? You'll keep her secret, but it's her business. You're not that excited about boys anyway.

7. The most important thing in a friendship is . . .

A. . . . helping each other through the bad times and caring for each other.

B. . . . giggling together, making up silly games, and generally having fun. The more friends the better!

C. . . . spending quality time with close friends and giving each other space to each do your own thing.

MOSTLY A's – CARER-SHARER

You are the one everyone turns to in a crisis. You are calm and kind and love to look after people and help them feel better. You don't have just one best friend, but are happiest in a group of several close friends. Beware: You may be a little oversensitive at times.

MOSTLY B's – PARTY PRINCESS

Your group of friends is always changing and getting bigger. You love to be the center of attention and love causing a commotion by being loud and silly. You see your friends as companions for fun, and try not to take anything too seriously. You may tend to be a little bit impatient sometimes, so try to chill out once in a while.

MOSTLY C's – MISS INDEPENDENT

You tend to have one best friend who is important to you, and if she's not around, you don't mind spending time on your own. You don't rely on others for things to do and generally don't mind what other people think of you. Sometimes you may be a little too unsociable, so try to venture out more.

HOW TO MAKE A FOUR-WAY FRIENDS' PIZZA

Take-out pizzas can be expensive, and getting everyone to agree on toppings can be a nightmare. Avoid the disputes and save money by getting three of your friends together to help make this delicious treat.

You will need:

- 2 cups self-rising flour • 1/2 teaspoon salt
- 4 tablespoons (1/2 stick) butter, cut into small pieces
- 1/4 cup milk and 1/4 cup water, combined
- 1/4 cup plus 1 tablespoon tomato pasta sauce • a variety of yummy toppings such as grated cheese, pepperoni, chopped ham, chopped mushrooms, sliced peppers, olives, pineapple chunks, etc.

1. Ask an adult to preheat the oven to 425°F.

2. Pour the flour into a large mixing bowl and then add the salt and the butter.

3. Rub the butter into the mixture by squashing it with flour between your fingers and then sprinkling it back into the bowl. Lift your fingers high above the flour. Do this until there are no lumps of butter and the mixture looks like bread crumbs.

4. Pour in half the milk-water mixture and stir with a table knife. When all the liquid has been absorbed, add more liquid until the mixture starts to stick together.

5. Get your hands into the bowl to squash your mixture into a soft dough. If your dough feels very sticky, add a little more flour.

6. Sprinkle some more flour onto your work surface and roll the dough into a large circle, about 1/2 inch thick, using a rolling pin. Then transfer it onto a baking sheet.

7. Spoon the pasta sauce onto your base and spread it out using the back of a spoon.

8. Now get creative: Divide the pizza into quarters and, with your friends, choose the toppings for each quarter. Finish with a layer of cheese before asking an adult to pop the pizza into the oven for 15 minutes.

9. Ask an adult to remove it from the oven. Let the pizza cool for about 10 minutes, and then enjoy.

THE GOLDEN RULES
OF FRIENDSHIP

Follow the golden rules of friendship to make sure you are friends forever.

THE RULES

DO laugh things off. You can solve a lot of problems if you don't take everything too seriously. Friends who can laugh together stay together.

DON'T be a gossip. Never say anything about your friend behind her back that you wouldn't say to her face – unless you are worried about her and are asking for some advice.

DO keep secrets secret. Your private conversations must always stay between the two of you – unless you think she might be in danger.

DON'T be a drama queen. Make sure you allow each other an equal amount of time to talk about your problems and what's going on in your lives.

DON'T steal what's hers — whether it's candy, ideas, clothes, or friends. If your friend doesn't want to share, respect her wishes.

DON'T pick on her faults — unless you are prepared to admit to your own. It is important to be honest with your friend, but only if you are prepared to be honest with yourself first.

DO keep changing. It is unrealistic to think that you and your friend will stay exactly the same forever and want to do the same things. If you always stick to the same routine when you see each other, you'll get bored.

DON'T say, "I told you so" — even if she does something you don't approve of. Do your best to put yourself in her shoes and support her even when she doesn't take your advice.

DO learn to forgive. It's easy to be angry with your friend when she hurts your feelings, and you may want to hurt her back. Make sure you listen to your friend's apology and forgive her if you think she means it. (See page 100.)

HOW TO MAKE A GROUP T-SHIRT

These fresh and funky T's are super fun to make. Wear them when you and your best friends go out together, and people will be able to spot your group from a mile away!

You will need:

- scrap paper • a clean white T-shirt each • cardboard
- a pencil • fabric pens • paintbrush • fabric paints

1. Get together with your friends and come up with a group name. Jot down some ideas on a piece of scrap paper. Your group name can be anything you like. For example, if you all love playing sports, you could be the Sporty Sistas. Or if you all love things that are girly and sparkly, you could call yourselves the Glam Stars. It doesn't matter what your name is, but you all have to agree on it.

2. Now decide on an emblem – a picture to represent your group. Make sure it is something that you can all draw and that fits with your group name. For instance, if you called your group the Glam Stars, you could choose a picture of a crown over a star, like this.

LET'S GET CRAFTY

3. Place the cardboard inside the T-shirt, so that the fabric is stretched flat. This will make it easier for you to draw your design onto it, and will keep the paint from going through to the other side.

4. Use a pencil to draw your emblem on the top right-hand corner of the front of your shirt, about 5 inches down from the shoulder. Write your group name in block letters underneath. Make sure it's big and noticeable.

5. With the cardboard still in place, go over your group name and the outline of your emblem with a fabric pen, then leave it to dry.

6. Use a paintbrush to fill in your emblem with fabric paint. Put your shirt aside to dry.

7. Once it's dry, turn your T-shirt over and design the back. Use a pencil to write your name or nickname (see page 16) across the shoulders of your shirt in bold letters, then draw your emblem (larger than you did on the front) underneath. Write your group name below.

8. Go over your group name and the outline of your emblem with a fabric pen and leave it to dry.

9. Paint in your emblem as you did before and leave it to dry.

10. To set your design so that your shirt can be worn and washed again and again, follow the instructions on the package of your fabric paints and pen. Most fabric paints are set by placing an old piece of cotton fabric on the design and ironing over it. Ask an adult to do this for you.

True-friend tip. Why not decorate your design even more? Simply glue sequins, buttons, or bows onto your shirt using fabric glue.

HOW TO BE FRIENDS WITH A VAMPIRE

Vampires might be dangerous, but let's face it, they're also pretty cool. They can fly, they wear stylish, dark-colored clothes, and they get to stay up as late as they want to every night. Follow these great tips to land yourself a brand-new bloodsucking buddy.

Know where they hang out. Check your local graveyards or any creepy mansions in the area. Stay away from the beach or the playground — all that sunshine is a killer for vampires' pale skin.

Avoid the local pizza parlor. This is garlic central, and vampires hate garlic. If you walk around smelling of garlic, you can guarantee vampires won't come anywhere near you.

Don't try to get your new pal to change her image. You will only hurt her vampire feelings. Vampires "live" for a very long time, so she may have been dressing like that for centuries.

Protect her identity. If you think your friend is a vampire, it's best to keep it to yourself. Some people get a little freaked out by the idea of being friends with the undead.

Don't bother trying to take her photograph. You won't be able to. True vampires can't be captured either digitally or on film, and most can't even be seen in mirrors.

Avoid going to sleepovers at her house. Sleepovers at vampires' houses aren't much fun, since they sleep (in coffins!) during the day. Invite her to stay over at your house instead. Having a friend who won't go to sleep can be very handy when you want to make a midnight snack.

HOW TO MAKE FRIENDSHIP COOKIES

People say that the way to a girl's heart is through her stomach, so make yourself really popular among your friends with a delicious batch of friendship cookies! Take a box of these when you're hanging out with your friends, and they'll soon be begging you to tell them the recipe.

You will need:

- 1 1/2 cups dry oatmeal
- 3/4 cup chocolate chips
- 1/4 cup soft brown sugar • 2 eggs
- 8 tablespoons (1 stick) softened butter

1. Ask an adult to preheat the oven to 375°F.

2. Combine the oatmeal, chocolate chips, and sugar in a large bowl and mix together well.

3. Crack the eggs into a small bowl by carefully tapping each one against the rim of the bowl until the shell cracks, then gently pulling the two halves apart.

4. Beat the eggs together with a fork until the yolks of the eggs are combined with the whites.

5. Stir the beaten eggs slowly into the oatmeal mixture, then gradually add the butter, stirring constantly until you have a rough dough.

6. Use your hands to make small balls out of the dough, then flatten them slightly onto a baking sheet.

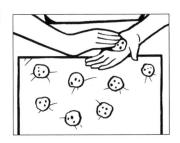

7. Ask an adult to put the baking sheet into the oven and bake for 8 minutes, or until golden brown.

8. Ask an adult to remove the cookies using oven mitts.

9. Let the cookies cool on the sheet for 2 minutes, then slide them off the sheet using a spatula. Put them in an airtight container to take to your friend's house.

True-friend tip. You don't really need an excuse to make cookies, but these little circles of goodness are perfect for spreading cheer among your friends. Scientists have proven that oatmeal and chocolate contain special chemicals

that can actually cheer you up when you are feeling blue. Why not give a plate to a friend who is feeling down? These yummy treats are sure to put a smile on her face.

WHY EVERYBODY NEEDS GOOD FRIENDS

You don't have to be the most popular girl at school or have an address book as fat as the telephone directory, but everyone should have a few special friends to share happy times and sad times with. Here's why:

Friendship is . . .

. . . telling each other your biggest fears and finding out that they are the same.

. . . laughing together at a joke that nobody else finds funny until tears stream down your faces and your sides hurt.

. . . discussing your deepest, darkest secrets and trusting that they will never be revealed to anyone else.

. . . knowing that your friend is unhappy, even before she tells you something is wrong.

. . . having someone who will let you know that your skirt is tucked into your underwear before anyone else sees you.

. . . sharing secrets as well as birthday cake.

. . . making plans for exciting things to do together on weekends and on school vacations.

. . . trusting that she won't laugh at you if you fall flat on your face, even if everyone else does.

. . . writing long letters or e-mails to each other when you are on vacation, even if you're not gone very long.

. . . having someone to share a large bucket of popcorn with at the movies.

. . . not being able to wait until the next day to talk, and calling each other as soon as you get home from school.

. . . having someone who knows you so well that it's a little scary. She even seems to know what you are going to say or do before you do.

. . . knowing that she will always be there for you, even if you mess up in a big way.

HOW TO MAKE A FRIENDSHIP FLOWER

Gather together a bunch of your best buddies to make a floral feel-good boost that will last for ages.

You will need:
- sheets of thin card stock in different colors • a small plate • a pencil • scissors • markers • a glue stick

1. Give each friend a sheet of card stock. Take turns placing the plate onto the card and drawing around it using a pencil.

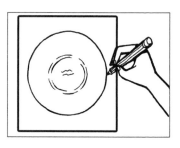

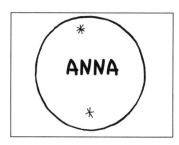

2. Cut out your circles. Each girl should take a marker and write her name across the middle of her circle. These will be the centers of your friendship flowers.

3. Cut out petals using the rest of the card stock. It is easiest to cut out one petal first and then use it as a template to draw around. Your petals can be any shape you like, but make sure there is enough room to write on them.

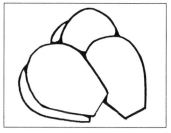

4. Once there are enough petals for each girl to have at least five, the floral fun can really begin. Choose one girl to go first and say her name out loud. Each girl then has to write down on a petal something that she thinks is fantastic about that person. It could be, "She can make the funniest faces," or, "She is amazing at soccer." When you are finished, hand the petals to the person in question.

5. Go around the group, doing the same thing for each friend in the group. Keep going until each girl has at least five petals in front of her.

6. Apply a thin layer of glue to the bottom of each petal and stick the petal to the back of the paper circle, so the petals' writing can be seen from the front, as shown below.

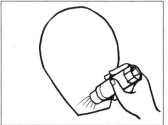

7. You can stick your flower on the wall at home or keep it somewhere safe and bring it out whenever you want to be reminded of what a special person you are.

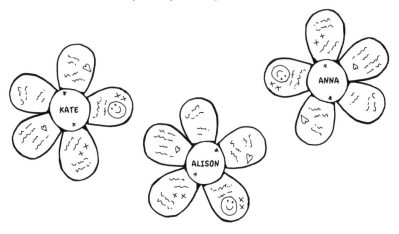

HOW TO USE "THE POWER OF PALS"

Friends are great for laughing and talking with, but did you know you can also use the power of your friendship to help you achieve your wildest dreams?

GOAL-GETTING GALS

Whether you are trying to save up your allowance to buy something special or are learning a difficult dance routine, some goals seem like they are out of reach. Here's how pal power can help:

1. Gather a group of friends who all have similar goals, and choose a day and a time to meet up each week for your "check-in" session. Monday at lunch is a good choice, so you can start the week with a positive attitude.

2. Share your goals with each other — small targets are fine! For example, you may want to grow your nails to the end of your fingertips. Agree on a date that you will all aim for to achieve your goals.

3. Make a chart in the back of a notebook with each of your friends' names across the top and the date of each check-in down the left-hand side. Add lines to make spaces to fill in how you are doing at each check-in.

4. At your check-in, take turns talking about your progress. Use this time to encourage each other and offer any tips you may think of. Record everyone's progress on your chart.

5. When you have reached the end of your chart, celebrate together, even if everyone hasn't quite reached her goal.

TWO HEADS ARE BETTER THAN ONE

Pal power can also help to make even the most boring assignments much easier and more fun. Each of you has different strengths — here's how to use those strengths to make your friendship an unstoppable force.

DO work together. When you have a project from school and you don't know where to start, arrange a "Brain Power Day." On this day, meet up with friends at your local library or at someone's house, and see what fun facts you can find out.

DO help each other. If you are really good at arithmetic but numbers freak your friend out, help her out with her math. In exchange, she can help you with something you struggle with and that she finds a breeze. This way, your homework will fly by, and you'll have fun at the same time.

DON'T copy each other's work. You won't learn that way, and you could end up getting into a lot of trouble with your teacher.

HOW TO MAKE A SUPERFAST FRIENDSHIP BRACELET

These cool and colorful bracelets are quick to make and fun to wear. Get together and create gifts that you and your friends will love.

You will need:

• a ruler • scissors • embroidery thread in five colors
• a binder clip • a piece of cardboard

1. Measure and cut a length of embroidery thread 18 inches long. Use this piece as a guide to cut a piece of each of the other colors to the same length.

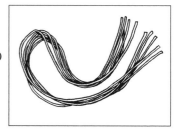

2. Hold all five pieces of thread together and fold them in half. Tie them together in a knot, leaving about 2 inches of loose ends.

3. Clip the knot onto your piece of cardboard with the binder clip, leaving the thread hanging down.

4. Separate out each color. Hook three colors around the index,

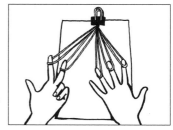

middle, and ring fingers on your right hand, then the two remaining colors around the index and middle fingers on your left hand.

5. Move the thread from the index finger on your right hand to the empty ring finger on your left hand, as shown. Keep the threads nice and taut so they don't get tangled.

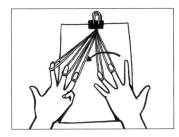

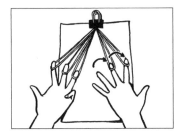

6. On your right hand, shift the threads up two fingers so that they are now on the index and middle fingers.

7. Now move the thread from the index finger on your left hand to the ring finger of your right hand. Keep pulling the threads out tightly.

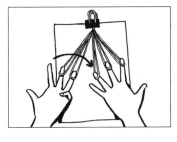

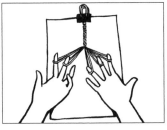

8. Repeat steps 5 to 7 and keep going until you are 2 inches away from the ends of your threads. Your bracelet should now be long enough to tie around your friend's wrist.

9. To finish, remove the bracelet from the clip and loop it around your friend's wrist. Secure it in place with a double knot.

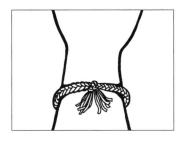

10. Once you and your friend have tied the bracelets around each other's wrists, try to keep them on for as long as possible, as a sign of your friendship.

IMAGINARY-FRIEND FUN

You've got best friends, pen pals, and maybe even friends who are boys. But did you know that you can have a great friendship with someone who doesn't exist outside your own head? Here are some reasons why imaginary friends are fabulous.

- You don't have to limit yourself to normal human friends. Why not make friends with a celebrity or even an animal?

- Your imaginary friend will never steal your style – you can dress her up any way you like and she won't argue with you.

- She'll be with you at all times. Every night can be a sleepover, and those terrifying thunderstorms won't be that scary anymore.

True-friend tip. Instead of keeping a diary, try writing your thoughts down as letters to your imaginary friend – you might find that you share a lot more. Of course, if you have a serious problem, talk to a real friend or adult.

HOW TO MAKE A FRIENDSHIP BOX

Give this special gift to a friend to promise her that you will always be there for her.

You will need:

• a large, empty matchbox* • a small photo of you and your friend together • a pencil • scissors • a glue stick • colored gift wrap • a small piece of colored paper • confetti • ribbon

1. Slide out the inner tray of your matchbox and place it on top of your photo. Draw around it using a pencil, then cut the photo out and glue it inside the bottom of the tray.

2. With your gift wrap pattern-side down in front of you, place the matchbox lengthwise in the bottom left-hand corner and draw around it. Slide the match-box up the paper so that the bottom edge sits on the top line

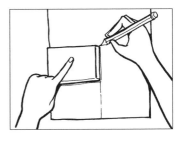

If you need to buy a full box of matches to get an empty box, ask an adult to empty the matches into a plastic bag and save them for another use.

and draw around it again. Repeat this once more so that you have one long rectangle made up of three matchbox shapes.

3. Cut out the long rectangle shape and then cover the plain side with a thin layer of glue.

4. Place the outer sleeve of your matchbox on the bottom edge of the long rectangle and wrap the paper around it neatly. Leave it to dry.

5. Meanwhile, take your small piece of writing paper and copy out this poem in your best handwriting. Or, if you're feeling creative, you can make up your own poem.

THE FRIENDSHIP POEM

Here inside this friendship box
A most important message lies.
I placed it here for you to find –
It's only for your eyes.

Treasure the note inside this box
And keep its message inside your heart.
It's a sign we'll be friends for life,
Nothing can ever make us part.

So if you're down and feeling blue,
This box was sent to say,
"Good times or bad, I'm here for you.
I promise that, today."

6. Fill the rest of the box with confetti that will spill out when your friend looks to see what is inside.

7. Slide the box inside the outer sleeve and then tie it up with ribbon in the same way you would tie up a gift box. Finish with a pretty bow.

True-friend tip. Why not give a friendship box to a friend to cheer her up if she is sad, or to say you are sorry if you have had an argument? And remember, if you are given one, you must look after it and treasure it forever as a sign of eternal friendship.

HOW TO HAVE THE ULTIMATE SLEEPOVER

Sometimes there aren't enough hours in the day to hang out with your friends, and that's why sleepovers were invented. Here are some handy hints for making yours a night to remember.

SLEEPOVER PARTY ESSENTIALS

DO have a dress code. Cute pajamas and the snuggliest socks are the height of sleepover chic.

DO play by your parents' rules. Keeping the noise down is the only surefire way of keeping your parents out of your hair for the evening.

DO make a sleepover playlist. Each guest should bring her favorite songs on her iPod or on CDs. Play the louder songs at the beginning of the night and save the quiet, mushy ones to play on low volume when you are supposed to be sleeping.

DO make sure you've got plenty of chocolate and candy. Ask each girl to bring some of her favorite treats, and then share and share alike.

DO pick out some cool DVDs to watch together. You can get scared, laugh, or cry together while watching!

DO try out new hairstyles on each other. Get each girl to bring along her brush and some cool clips, headbands, or curlers and then go wild. The great thing about a sleepover is that no one will see your hairstyle if it looks crazy.

DON'T miss midnight! It's the best hour for spilling secrets and devouring snacks.

DON'T forget magazines. Get each girl to bring as many current and old issues of her favorites as she can carry so that you can all flip through and decide who your number one superstar is.

DON'T be too shy about your crush. Sleepovers are a great time to confide in your friends and come up with a plan of action. But remember — don't share your friends' secrets with others after the sleepover if you don't want them sharing yours!

WHEN IS A FRIEND NOT A TRUE FRIEND?

Some people can seem like they're your friends, but they're nowhere to be seen when you need a shoulder to cry on. Here's how to tell a true friend from a fake friend.

A TRUE FRIEND WOULD NEVER . . .

. . . persuade you to do something you don't want to do — whether it is something embarrassing to entertain her, or something that you think is wrong.

What to do. Try to stand up to her and explain that a real friend wouldn't want you to do anything that would make you feel uncomfortable. If she doesn't listen, steer clear and find a true friend who will like you for who you are.

A TRUE FRIEND WOULD NEVER . . .

. . . turn other friends against you. If one friend has decided she doesn't want to be your friend anymore, she might try to keep other people from hanging around with you, too.

What to do. Try speaking to your friends one-on-one to explain what is happening. If they don't want to know, ditch them — you don't want to be friends with people like that anyway. If it is happening to you, it is sure to be happening to someone else, too. Look out for girls going through the same thing as you and become friendly with them.

A TRUE FRIEND WOULD NEVER . . .

. . . put you down in public. If your friend makes nasty comments or jokes about you in front of other people, it can make you feel small and very silly. It might seem like she is just trying to be funny, but if she is hurting your feelings, then she is not acting like a true friend.

What to do. Wait until you are alone with your friend and explain to her how she is making you feel. She may not have realized that she was hurting your feelings and might promise never to do it again. If she still doesn't stop, try to spend less time with her, and spend more time with other, truer, friends.

A TRUE FRIEND WOULD NEVER . . .

. . . borrow your things without asking or take money from you. Everyone likes to help their friends out by sharing and maybe even treating them to some candy if they don't have any allowance left, but they should never make you feel bad by hassling you.

What to do. Confide in an adult whom you trust.

A TRUE FRIEND WOULD NEVER . . .

. . . reveal your secrets. Friendship is all about trusting each other, and it can feel terrible when you feel like the trust between you has been broken.

What to do. Ask your friend why she revealed your secret and remind her that you only told her on the understanding she would not tell anyone else. If she is sorry, forgive her, but be careful about telling her any secrets in the future until you are sure that she is able to keep them.

True-friend tip. Girls can sometimes treat their closest friends badly to make others like them more. They do this because they feel unhappy or insecure, but it isn't a fair way to behave. If you have tried to speak to your friend about how she is upsetting you and she doesn't stop, she doesn't deserve your friendship.

Friends are there to make life better and more fun. If a friend makes you feel bad, perhaps it's time to make a new friend.

YOU KNOW YOU SPEND TOO MUCH TIME TOGETHER WHEN . . .

Being best friends is awesome, but did you know that there is such a thing as spending too much time together? No? Answer true or false to the statements below to find out if you and your friend are in danger of becoming a terrible two-headed monster.

TRUE OR FALSE?

- Her parents automatically set you a place at the table for dinner, even when you're not there.

- You cry every time your friend goes on vacation. It feels like nothing this tragic has ever happened to you before.

- You show up at parties wearing identical outfits, completely unplanned.

- When someone asks a question, you answer the same thing at the same time.

- Your mom and dad have her school picture next to yours on the mantel.

- You know your friend is going to call even before your phone rings.

- Your handwriting is exactly the same as hers.

- Your other friends merge your names into one – for example, if your names are Jessie and Lucy, they call you Juicy, or Katy and Emma and they call you Kemma.

- New people you meet can't believe you're not sisters.

THE RESULTS

If your answer was "true" to four or more of the statements above, you and your friend are spending too much time together and are in danger of merging into one monstrous two-headed being. You need to take action before it's too late.

WHAT TO DO

It is great to be best friends, but it is important to have your own identity, too. Good friends let each other be themselves and value each other's differences rather than trying to be exactly the same all of the time. Try taking up different hobbies – this will not only give you more to talk about when you see each other, but it will also help you make some new pals.

HOW TO MAKE A FRIENDSHIP FORTUNE-TELLER

Find out what the future has in store for you and your friends with this funky fortune-teller.

You will need:

- 1 sheet of 8 1/2 x 11-inch paper • scissors • a pen
- markers or colored pencils

1. With the longest side of the paper at the bottom, fold the top right-hand corner of the paper so that the right-hand edge lies along the bottom edge. This will leave you with a rectangle of paper on the left-hand side. Trim this off using your scissors. You should now have a folded triangle of paper.

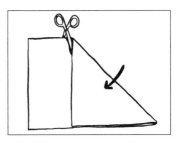

True-friend tip. To make your fortune-teller superneat, smooth down each fold you make firmly with your fingertips.

2. With the longest side of the triangle at the bottom, fold the triangle in half so that the right-hand corner completely covers the left-hand corner. Smooth down the fold.

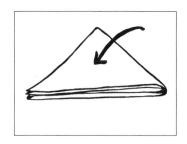

3. Repeat step 2 to make an even smaller triangle.

4. Open up your triangle to reveal a square of paper with lots of creases running through a central point.

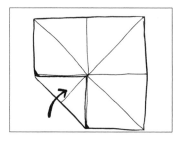

5. Using the creases as a guide, fold this square into a smaller one by folding each corner of the square into the center point.

6. Turn your paper over and repeat step 5 to make an even smaller square.

7. Turn your square over. You should be able to see four square flaps of paper. Color each of these flaps a different color using your markers or colored pencils.

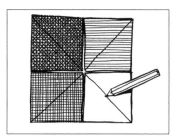

8. Turn your square over again and write a single number from 1 to 8 in each of the triangles you can see.

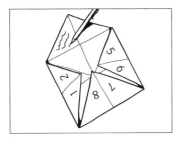

9. Unfold the top triangle and write one friendship fortune on each side of the crease. Your fortunes can be whatever you like, but keep them mysterious and fun. Here are some you could try:

- Wear something pink and you will make a new friend.
- On Tuesday, someone you love will misunderstand you.
- Beware of frogs and toads — they may not be all they seem.

Repeat this for each of the triangular flaps until you have written eight friendship fortunes, then fold all the flaps back to the center to make a square.

10. Fold your square in half lengthwise to make a rectangle with two of your colored flaps showing on each side.

11. Pull each of the four flaps out using your thumbs and index fingers, and push the tips up and into the middle.

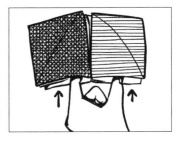

FUN WITH FORTUNES

To use your finished fortune-teller, hold it with your thumbs and index fingers together so that all four of the colored flaps are showing. Ask your friend to pick a color. To find her fortune, open and close the fortune-teller once in each direction for each letter in the word. For instance, if your friend picks "BLUE," open and close the fortune-teller four times. Ask your friend to pick a number from the inner flaps that she can see. Open and close the fortune-teller this number of times. Ask her to choose another number. Lift the flap with this number on it to reveal your friend's fortune.

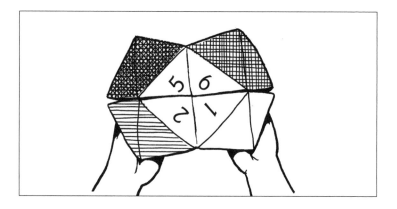

True-friend tip. Fortune-tellers are easy to make, so why not make lots for different areas of your life? You could make one about love with fortunes such as, "A supercute boy will offer to lend you his bike," or one about school. That one could include fortunes like "Make sure to finish all your homework this week."

FIVE REASONS WHY PETS MAKE GREAT FRIENDS

Reason one. Walking the dog is excellent exercise and a great way to get out for some fresh air.

Reason two. A cat is the perfect TV companion – it'll keep your lap warm but never talk through your favorite show.

Reason three. You can't share candy with pets, because it makes them sick. What a shame – more candy just for you!

Reason four. Your pets will never disagree with you or laugh at you when you do something silly, but they will always be on hand for a cuddle when you're feeling blue.

Reason five. You can whisper all your secrets to your pets and be sure they'll never tell (unless you have a talking parrot, of course).

REAL FRIENDS OR FAKE FRIENDS?

Real friends are friends you can trust to always be there for you. Fake friends will be around while everything is fun, but they'll be nowhere to be seen when the going gets tough. Here's how to tell a real friend from a fake one.

A REAL FRIEND SAYS . . .	A FAKE FRIEND SAYS . . .
• "Of course you can borrow my favorite top."	• "What will you give me in return?"
• "What's up? You can talk to me about it if you want."	• "Oh, just cheer up, will you?"
• "I promise you can trust me."	• "Ooh, tell me — I love secrets, they're so exciting!"

• "I would love it if you'd come to my birthday party!"

• "We'll meet you in the park, by the swings, at 3 P.M."

• "You can come to my birthday party only if you bring your new karaoke machine/cool older sister, etc."

• "Um . . . yeah . . . we'll probably meet you in the park at some point later. . . ."

HOW TO SEAL YOUR FRIENDSHIP

A ritual is a ceremony that is made up of special words and actions, performed in a specific order. Performing a friendship ritual will seal your friendship and bring good luck to you and your friends. This one is for two or more people to perform together.

You will need:

• a clean tablecloth or blanket • each friend to bring a personal item, such as a favorite photograph or a homemade gift • some juice • a cup for each friend

SETTING THE SCENE

Lay the tablecloth on the ground. Somewhere outdoors is best, such as the corner of your backyard or under a tree in the park.

Ask each friend to lay her chosen item in the center of the cloth and then to take a seat beside her item on the cloth.

LET THE SIPPING BEGIN

Pour a little juice into each of the cups and then ask everyone to raise her cup for a toast. Together, recite this phrase:

> "With the sharing of this drink, we agree
> to share our lives together forevermore."

PUT YOUR HEART INTO IT

Now it is time to pass your personal items around the group. The item could be a favorite photograph or even a friendship box (see page 43) or a friendship bracelet (see page 40). Ask each girl to pick up her personal item from the cloth and pass it to the girl on her left. The girl giving the item should make the following promise:

> "This *insert name of item here* is a symbol of who I am.
> By giving it to you, I promise that you will have
> a piece of my heart forever."

After these words have been spoken, the girl receiving the item should say:

"I accept this *insert name of item here* as a symbol of who
you are, and promise to treasure it and
your friendship forever."

THE SACRED RING

When all the items have been exchanged, ask your friends to link hands and close their eyes to chant the oath of friendship below.

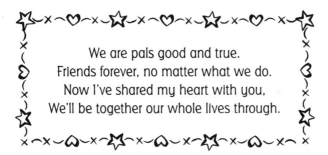

We are pals good and true.
Friends forever, no matter what we do.
Now I've shared my heart with you,
We'll be together our whole lives through.

True-friend tip. Ask each friend to try to memorize the words before the ceremony.

FRIENDS FOREVER

Each time you have an argument or a falling-out after this, remember this ritual and how you felt when you made these promises to one another. It will make it much easier to forgive one another and continue being friends.

HOW TO MAKE A PERSONALIZED BIRTHDAY CARD

Instead of buying a generic card from a store, transform an old one into the perfect personalized card. Give your friend a card she will REALLY like for her next birthday.

You will need:

• an old birthday card • a sharp pencil • modeling clay
• scissors • a photo of your friend • old newspapers or
magazines • tape • one sheet of plain paper • a glue stick

1. Consider what parts of the card you could replace with new pictures. Make a hole in the parts of the card you have chosen by pushing a sharp pencil through the card into a lump of modeling clay underneath.

2. Remove the pencil and clay, and carefully insert the point of your scissors into the hole you have just made. Cut out the areas of the card that will become your windows.

3. Choose a nice photo of your friend and some photos of her favorite celebrity or animal from old magazines. Check that they are the right size to show through the windows by placing the card over them. Cut the photos out, leaving a little extra around the edges.

4. Position your pictures behind the windows in the front of your card and then tape them down on the inside cover of the card.

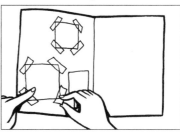

5. Lay your card out flat on a sheet of plain paper and draw around it using your pencil. Lift the card off and cut the shape out so that you have a piece of paper the same size as your card.

6. Apply a thin layer of glue to the inside of your card and the piece of paper. Stick the paper onto the inside of the card to cover up the tape and any old messages.

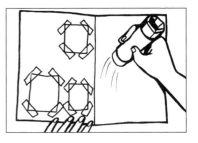

7. When the glue has dried, write in your very own birthday greeting. The card is ready to give to your friend.

True-friend tips. Don't stop at birthdays. Use this method to make cards for your friends for Christmas or other holidays. Why not put yourself into some really funny scenes to cheer your friend up when she is down? Be careful not to give your friend a card that she's already given you, though. And if you're using an old birthday card with an age on the front, make sure it is the age that your friend is about to be!

HOW TO "GO FISH" FOR FRIENDS

Here's a fun card game that you can make at home, which you not only can play with your friends, but which features them as part of the game, too.

You will need:

- 3 sheets of 8 1/2 x 11-inch card stock or thick paper
- a pen • a glue stick • 4 photographs (one of you, and three of your friends) • lots of old magazines and/or a computer and printer • scissors • colored markers

1. Take a sheet of card stock and divide it into eight equal rectangles by folding it in half once lengthwise, and then twice widthwise. Unfold and repeat with the other two sheets.

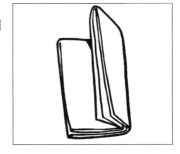

2. On one of your sheets of card stock write your name at the top of one of the rectangles. Write the names of your three best friends at the top of each of three other rectangles.

3. Use a glue stick to put your picture under your name and the pictures of each of your friends underneath their names.

4. Underneath each picture, write the following headings: "Fave color," "Fave animal," "Fave food," "Fave celeb," "Fave hobby," and then write in what each of these favorites are for yourself and each friend.

5. Go through all of your old magazines, to look for and cut out the pictures for each of your friends' favorite things that match all of the headings listed in step **4** (except favorite color). If you can't find them all, check the Internet. Once you have found as many pictures as possible, ask a parent or whoever owns the computer if it would be okay for you to print them out.

6. Once you have as many pictures as you can find, you can start filling in the rest of your rectangles. Glue each picture into the center of a rectangle, write the name of the person whose favorite it is across the top of the card, and label it underneath. For example: "Anna" across the top, and "Fave hobby: Karate" underneath.

7. For any pictures that you can't find, simply draw a picture of your friend's favorite thing and then color it in.

8. For the favorite color cards, write each name on the top of a card and then use markers in each person's chosen color to draw a squiggle in the center of the card. Label the color underneath.

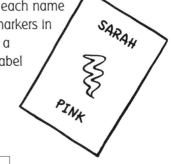

9. When you have filled in all the rectangles on each of your sheets of card stock, cut them out so that you have 24 separate cards.

True-friend tip. To make your cards last for lots of games, cover both sides of each of the sheets of card stock with clear contact paper before cutting them out.

TO PLAY THE GAME

You will need between two and six players.

1. Shuffle your cards and deal three cards to each player. Put the rest in a stack in the middle, facedown.

2. Each player should look at the cards she has, but hide them from the other players. The aim of the game is to collect a full set – six cards – for as many friends as possible.

3. The player on the left of the dealer starts. She (Player 1) must ask another player in the circle (Player 2) for a particular card that she needs. For example, if Player 1 already has Claire's photo card and Claire's favorite color card, she might ask, "Do you have Claire's favorite food?"

4. If Player 2 has that card, she must hand it over, and Player 1 has another turn. If Player 2 does not have this card, she must say, "Go fish," and Player 1 draws one card from the stack of cards in the middle. Then the player to the left of Player 1 takes her turn as in step **3.**

5. When any player gets a full set, she should put it down in front of her, faceup. The game continues until either someone has no cards left in her hand or the stack in the middle runs out. The player who collects the most full sets wins.

True-friend tip. Listen very carefully to what your friends ask for when it is their turn. This will give you clues as to what they have in their hands and what you could ask them for when it is your turn.

HOW TO DRAW A SILHOUETTE OF YOUR FRIEND

Drawing silhouettes is an easy way to make a really cool piece of artwork in an exact likeness of your friend. Take turns posing for a silhouette, using the instructions below.

You will need:

• 3 sheets of 11 x 17-inch white paper • 2 sheets of 11 x 17-inch black paper • a pencil • a lamp • scissors • adhesive putty • a glue stick

1. Stick a sheet of white paper to the wall using adhesive putty (check with a parent first to see if it is okay to use it on the wall you wish to use).

2. Position your lamp so that it will shine directly onto the paper.

3. If it is daytime, close the curtains and try to block as much natural light out of the room as possible. If you are doing this in the evening, turn off all the lights other than your lamp.

4. Ask your friend to stand or sit sideways in front of the lamp.

5. Move the lamp around until you can see your friend's shadow very clearly on the piece of paper.

6. Use a pencil to very carefully draw all the way around the outline of your friend's shadow.

7. Take the sheet of paper down and cut the shape of your friend's silhouette out to make a template.

8. Place your template on a piece of black paper and draw around it. Cut this out.

9. Glue the black silhouette onto a fresh sheet of white paper using a glue stick.

10. Now ask your friend to draw your silhouette following steps 1 to 7.

11. Stick the white silhouette of you directly onto a sheet of black paper. This way, your picture will contrast with your friend's picture.

12. Mount your works of art in pretty frames or simply stick them up on your wall using the adhesive putty.

True-friend tip. Why stop at black and white? Experiment with different, cool color combinations for a really funky work of art. A hot pink silhouette on a blue background would look great, or even one cut from patterned gift wrap.

HOW TO HOLD A FRIENDSHIP AWARD CEREMONY

An award ceremony is a cool way of showing your friends how much you care about them. It can take place at someone's party or a sleepover, or you can even just get everyone together one day after school.

PLANNING

First you have to think up the categories. Here are some ideas:

Funniest friend

Best listener

Smartest friend

Most loyal friend

Best friend at giving advice

Sportiest friend

Fairest friend

Most patient friend

You and another friend can make up the judging panel. To make it fair, only one prize can be awarded to each friend, and everyone should get a prize. Write your choices down on a piece of paper and keep them secret and safe until the ceremony.

PRIZES

For your awards, you need something extra special that your friends can all wear with pride. These badges are perfect, and they're very easy to make.

You will need:
- a piece of thin white paper • a pencil • a sheet of colored card stock • scissors • a glitter pen • safety pins • tape

1. Place the piece of thin white paper on top of the star shape pictured here and carefully trace around it using your pencil. Cut it out. This is your template.

2. Place the paper star template in the bottom left-hand corner of your colored card stock. Draw around it using your pencil.

3. Move your template to the right and draw around it again. Repeat this until your whole sheet is filled with star shapes. Cut them all out. These are your badges.

4. On each badge, write the name of the winner and the award with a glitter pen. For example: "Molly, Funniest Friend."

5. When the writing is dry, attach a safety pin carefully to the back of each star with tape. Make sure you tape down the curved side of the pin rather than the pointy end.

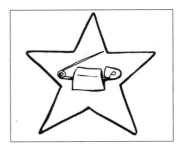

True-friend tip. To make your award badges superspecial, decorate them with blobs of glitter glue and sequins.

AND THE WINNER IS . . .

During the ceremony, present the correct badge to each winner. You should give your reasons for your choices — for example, "Nina was chosen as the Best Friend at Giving Advice because she is a great problem-solver. She's also always willing to help a friend in need."

THE FRIENDSHIP DOCTOR

Dr. Bigheart specializes in taking your ailing friendships and making them healthy. Here are her answers to some of the most common friendship dilemmas.

Dear Dr. Bigheart,

There's a girl in my class who everyone ignores. I feel sorry for her and would like to make friends with her, but I'm worried that if I do that, my own friends will laugh at me and start to ignore me, too.

DR. BIGHEART SAYS . . .

Don't worry about things that haven't even happened yet. If you want to start including this girl, do it, but take it one step at a time. Making an effort to smile and say hello to her in the mornings is a good place to start. Then try including her in conversations when she is nearby. If you do this casually, your friends will not feel threatened or worry that you are going off with this other girl. They'll probably leave you to it. Good for you for being so considerate of this girl's feelings — your friends should copy your example!

Dear Dr. Bigheart,

My friends seem to get a lot more allowance than I do, and their parents always seem to be buying them new clothes. I feel really uncool compared to them—it's not fair.

DR. BIGHEART SAYS . . .

Being cool is not about money and clothes. Your friends must think you're pretty cool to like you in the first place, regardless of how much money is in your purse. If you want a new look, why not go through your wardrobe and try out new combinations? Remember, being cool is based on who you are, not what you buy or what you wear. You have your own value and strengths, whether it's making people laugh or coming up with new ideas. Stay strong!

Dear Dr. Bigheart,

One of my best friends has been acting very strangely lately. She keeps going off and sitting on her own at lunchtime and seems so moody. She used to be really chatty, but now she's always quiet. Do you think I've done something wrong?

DR. BIGHEART SAYS . . .

It sounds to me as if your friend has a big problem on her mind, and it doesn't necessarily have to do with you. Perhaps she has some problems at home that she feels too upset to talk about. Try to pull her aside and let her know that you are worried about her. Ask her if there is anything you can do to help. If she refuses to talk, it may be worth talking to a teacher or other adult who you know and trust, and telling him or her about how she has changed. The adult may be able to find out what is wrong. Good luck, and well done for being such a caring friend!

HOW TO MAKE A CLUBHOUSE

Make your own clubhouse so you and your friends will have a cool place to hang out without being interrupted by pesky adults. Here's how to set it up.

FIND YOUR LOCATION

You'll need somewhere with enough room for all of you to sit down and for your supplies, too. How about an attic? A corner of your bedroom? Any spot you can call your own will do.

CUSTOMIZE AND COZY IT UP

To make your clubhouse look gorgeous, you'll need to get creative. Here are some ideas:

- Put a big bulletin board up on the wall so that you can cover it with posters and change the pictures easily to show who and what you're into that week.

- Buy, beg, or borrow some strings of lights to make your clubhouse instant girly heaven.

- Keep a big box marked "supplies" that's packed with a secret stash of goodies: juice or soda, candy, magazines, and games.

- And, of course, you'll each need somewhere to sit down, so why not make personalized covers for floor cushions?

HOW TO MAKE FLOOR CUSHIONS

You will need:

- fabric • an old cushion or pillow • scissors • straight pins
- a needle • thread in a color similar to your fabric
- old newspaper • fabric paint • a paintbrush
- buttons and sequins • fabric glue

1. Cut out a piece of fabric that is twice the size of your cushion, with an extra 2 inches added to its length and width.

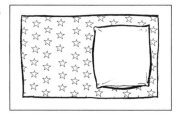

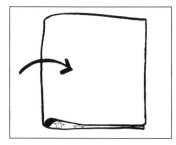

2. Fold the fabric in half. If it is patterned, make sure the pattern side is on the inside.

3. Pin the edges of your fabric together using straight pins, leaving one side of your square open.

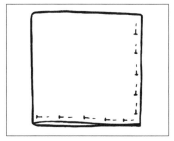

4. Thread your needle with 5 feet of thread and tie a double knot at the end. Push the needle through the bottom left-hand corner of the cushion cover and pull through up to the knot.

5. Sew along this outer edge in a straight line, no more than 1/2 inch in from the edge. Use small stitches, and try to keep them close together.

6. Continue sewing until you are about 1/2 inch from the corner. Turn the corner and sew along as you did in step 5 with the other pinned side of the cushion. When you reach the top right-hand corner, secure your stitches by sewing over the same spot ten times. Cut off any excess thread.

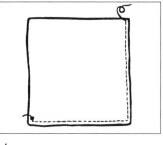

7. Turn the cushion cover inside out and place a piece of newspaper inside to protect the other side of the fabric.

8. Decorate your cushion with fabric paints. You could paint on your group emblem (see page 27) or whatever you like. Make sure you mark your cushion with your name or initials so everyone

knows whom it belongs to. When you have finished, glue on your sequins and your buttons and then leave it to dry.

9. Insert your cushion and sew up the final side by folding the loose edges inside 1/2 inch and then pinning both sides together. Sew this side up over the pins just as you did before.

True-friend tip. Once your clubhouse is complete, why not ask your parents if you can use it as the venue for an awesome sleepover party (see page 46)?

HOW TO MAKE UP AFTER AN ARGUMENT

So, it's happened – you and your friend had a disagreement that turned into a fight, and before you knew it, the two of you weren't speaking anymore. It can happen very easily! But there's no need to stop being friends – you just need to learn the art of making up.

MAKE HER LAUGH

Making her laugh is a foolproof option. If she's a good friend, you'll have a decent idea of what is guaranteed to make her chuckle. Get it right, and she won't have any choice but to let that frown melt into a bout of giggles. Here are some ideas:

- Catch her eye and make your silliest face.

- Call her up and sing a silly song over the phone.

- Ask her if she remembers the hilarious time when . . .

WRITE HER A "SORRY" CARD

If you feel that you were in the wrong in the argument, choose or make a card with "Sorry" on the front. Inside, write your apology straight from the heart. Explain your reasons for doing what you did and say that you hope she will forgive you and move on.

TREAT HER WELL

Nothing wins a friend back better than being nice. Spend time with her, make her a friendship card, or even lend her your brand-new top.

HOW TO MAKE A FRIENDSHIP TIME CAPSULE

You might not believe it now, but when you are old and gray you may find it hard to remember all the fun you had with your friends when you were younger. Make a time capsule filled with mementos to remind yourself of the good times you are having together right now.

You will need:

• a cookie tin • acrylic paints in various colors • a permanent marker • a collection of mementos and messages from you and your friends • a sheet of paper and an envelope for each of you • some pens • masking tape

1. Wash out your cookie tin with soapy water. Rinse it and leave it to dry.

2. Paint the outside of the tin and the lid in a light color, such as pale blue or yellow, and then leave it to dry. Use acrylic paints for this, as these will stick better to the outside of the tin.

3. Decorate the inside base of the tin by painting on a pretty pattern. You could paint a heart or flowers or even use your friendship emblem (see page 27). When you are finished, put the tin aside to dry.

4. On the lid of the tin, use your permanent marker to write in bold letters the date when you want to open your capsule, far in the future. For example, you could write, "DO NOT OPEN UNTIL AUGUST 2050." Leave it to dry.

5. Meanwhile, choose the items that you are going to put into the capsule. Think of the memories you want to preserve for the future. Good things to put into your friendship time capsule include:

- photographs of all of you together
- pictures of your favorite singers and movie stars
- programs and mementos from things you have done together, such as plays you have acted in or been to together, old movie tickets from seeing your favorite films, or newspaper cuttings about sporting events you have attended.

6. Give a piece of paper, an envelope, and a pen to each of your friends and ask them to write a letter to be read aloud to the group when the time capsule is opened. The letters can be about anything you like – they could include, for example, a story about a fun time you have shared together or what you like best about each of your friends. You could even write about what you hope you and each of your friends will be doing when you open the box.

7. When you have all finished your letters, ask your friends to put them into the envelopes and seal them.

8. Gather together all of the letters and put them inside your friendship time capsule with the collection of mementos.

9. Put the lid on the capsule and seal it shut by covering over the seam between the tin and the lid with lots of layers of masking tape.

10. Ask each friend to write her initials on the tape, using a permanent marker. This way you will all know that no one has snuck a peek inside the capsule before you come to open it.

11. Hide the time capsule somewhere it will not be found for many years. This could be in the attic, at the back of your closet, or under your bed. You could even ask your parents' permission to dig a hole and bury it in the backyard.

True-friend tip. Don't forget to take the capsule with you if you move to a new house. The new owners of your house might not take kindly to a bunch of ladies banging on their door in forty years' time, demanding to look for a time capsule in their attic.

HOW TO MAKE FRIENDS WITH YOURSELF

Did you know that you have already met the person who knows you best in the world? Someone who will always be there for you and will always take the time to listen to your problems and cheer you up. Follow these great tips to make friends with and look after the best pal you will ever have – YOU.

- Don't take things too seriously. If you feel grumpy, slap a big smile on your face. You'll find it hard to be grouchy while you're smiling.

- Write yourself a list of five good things you've done at the end of each week. It could be anything from making a new friend to getting an A at school.

- Be a friend to your body. Don't spend all your spare time in front of the TV or computer – go outside and get some exercise.

- Give yourself a pat on the back every time you achieve something. After all, that's what you'd expect a friend to do.

- Spend some quality time with yourself. Learn how to enjoy yourself even if you're not hanging out with friends. You can use the time to read, get creative, or just chill out – you deserve it!

HOW TO MAKE FRIENDS WITH A CELEBRITY

The life of a star can seem so glamorous – parties, award ceremonies, and international fame – but celebrities are still just normal people! Here's how to become friends with a celeb.

DON'T get too starstruck. When you spot a star, try to stay calm. This can be tricky when your stomach is doing somersaults, but if you treat celebrities like you would normal people, they are more likely to want to become your friends.

DO make them laugh. Instead of immediately asking about the latest movie or song they worked on, why not try asking them a silly, random question to make them laugh? Try, "Do you dunk your cookies in milk or just eat them plain?" or "Which do you prefer, sharks or dolphins?" Your idol will be so pleased to have the chance to talk about something other than his or her career that he or she will warm to you right away.

DO be loyal. Just like your other friends, celebrities are going to be your friend only if you are genuine. If they suspect you are interested in them only because of the fun parties they can get you into, they will move on before you can say "VIP area, please."

DO join their fan club. Not only will you get special access to their official Web sites, but you will receive information on where your celebrity will be appearing next before anybody else does. That means you will be first in line for an autograph, and therefore have a better chance to talk to him or her.

DO write letters or send e-mails to your favorite stars. This will not only let them know that you care, but some celebrities have even been known to write back.

DON'T be too upset if they don't write back, or just send a form letter. Celebrities are very busy people and may not have time to answer every message.

DO get friendly with up-and-coming stars. Let's be honest, ending up best pals with a Hollywood A-lister is a little unlikely. But maybe you know a really good actor who you think might hit the big time. Get on his or her holiday card list now, before it's too late!

HOW TO GIVE A MAD-CAP MAKEOVER

Getting together and giving each other mad-cap makeovers is a lot of fun and a great opportunity to play around with the way you look. First, ask an adult's permission. Then, use any or all of these crazy makeover ideas to create some seriously "stylish" looks.

HAIR-RAISING IDEAS

Sit your friend down in a chair with her back to you and stand behind her. Ask her to brush through her hair first to get rid of any tangles, and then get stylin'. Here are some ideas:

For long locks – bigger is bolder. Start with dry hair and backcomb sections of her hair to create a wild, shaggy look.

To backcomb, take a section of hair about an inch wide and hold it above her head with your left hand. Take a comb in your right hand and hold it about an inch up from the roots. In short strokes, gently comb the hair toward her scalp until it begins to fluff up. Be careful not to pull. Do this on a few sections on the top of her head, then smooth the rest of her hair over the top.

For short styles – the spike is right. Start with wet hair and use hair gel or wax to sculpt your friend's hair into crazy spikes and shapes, then leave it to dry. Finish with a generous spritz of glitter spray.

True-friend tip. Use hair mascara in bright, contrasting colors to make eye-catching stripes all over your friend's hair.

Warning. Unless you want to lose a friend and/or risk a serious grounding, do not under any circumstances pick up a pair of scissors and start cutting her hair. Haircutting should be left to professionals. You should also never use hair dye without getting an adult's permission.

CLASHING CLOTHES

Ask each of your friends to bring some of their clothes over, and create some cool new outfits by mixing and matching each others' styles. Here are a few ideas:

All bright now. Try combining all the brightest items of clothing to make one crazy, clashing, colorful outfit.

Crazy for patterns. Checks, stripes, polka dots – throw them all together to create a weird and wacky look that will make your head spin if you look at it for too long.

More, more, more. Don't forget the accessories – the more bling the better. You could go for lots of bangles or bracelets, large rings, and chunky pendants.

MIND-BLOWING MAKEUP

Forget "the natural look" and get ready to make a statement. Ask your mom very nicely if she has any extra makeup you can have, pick up some free samples from cosmetics counters, or buy some inexpensive makeup. But remember, don't ever share makeup – it's unhygienic!

Eye-catching eyes. Using a bright eye shadow, gently smudge color over your friend's eyelids, right up to her eyebrows. This will give her an extreme, rocker-chick look.

Look-at-me lips. Use a shocking pink or red lipstick, and make a statement with your friend's lips. Experiment with lip shapes and colors.

Check-me-out cheeks. Whether you choose a golden bronze shade or a pretty pink blush, brush it onto your friend's face. Do it in sweeps starting from her cheek and moving up into her hairline, or in little rosy circles on each of her cheeks, for a doll-like look.

THE BIG REVEAL

Finally, show her how she looks in the mirror, and get ready for her to get her revenge on you once she has stopped giggling. Take lots of pictures of each other looking your silliest, but remember to get yourselves looking back to normal again before you leave the house.

HOW TO CREATE YOUR OWN "FRIENDSPEAK"

Let's face it — there are times when you need to keep your conversations private, whether it's to stop your little brother from eavesdropping or to discuss your latest crush. There is only one surefire way to be certain your chats don't become the subject of a school scandal or family dinner-table discussions, and that's to switch to "friendspeak."

INGENIOUS INITIALS

Talk to your friends and come up with a set of codes to use when you need to discuss private things in public places. A quick and simple way of doing this is to take the initials of the person you are talking about, and use two different words starting with those letters.

So Mark Hill could become Monsieur Horse and Robert Johnston could become Raspberry Jelly.

This is an easy way to keep identities a closely guarded secret.

CRYPTIC CLUES

Describe people and places without actually saying the names. The swings in the park could be "the dangly chain seats," the candy store could be "the source of all things sweet and lovely," and school could be "the house of major dullness." Your parents could be "the old squad" or "the noseys." Now invent some of your own!

THE "FRIENDSPEAK" DICTIONARY

Use the words below to confuse nearby adults and anyone not in your gang so that you can talk freely without being understood.

WORD	MEANING	EXAMPLE
Delicious	Good-looking	"Alex looks so delicious today."
Offside	Amazing	"That film was totally offside."
Celery	Boring	"Assembly was so celery."
Cash in!	Yes, definitely!	"Pizza for lunch? Cash in!"
Log off	No way	"Wear my pink top? Log off."
Simmer	Calm down	"It's not that bad. Simmer."

THE DOS AND DON'TS OF SAFE FRIENDSHIPS

Whether you are out and about with old friends or online with new ones, it's important to be aware of your personal safety so that you can have fun without putting yourself in any danger. Here are a few things you can do to make sure your friendships are safe:

DON'T give out any personal details when you are chatting online. Personal details include: your full name, your school, details about any of your friends, and any part of your address other than your town. If anyone pesters you for this or wants to meet you, log off right away and let an adult you trust know about it.

DO stand up for yourself. **DON'T** be encouraged to do things that you wouldn't normally do just because everyone else is doing it.

DO tell your parents exactly where you'll be when you go out. This isn't just so they can have control over your life — it's because they need to know where you are if you don't get back on time.

DON'T confuse harmless mischief and real trouble. Playing silly games and pranks is exciting, but getting involved in activities that could cause danger or upset you or anyone else is serious stuff.

DO trust your "gut instinct." This is the feeling you get when you know something that's happening is not right. If you think you should leave a situation or tell an adult, then do so right away.

REASONS WHY BOYS MAKE GOOD FRIENDS, TOO

You might think they're noisy and smelly, and you might go out of your way to avoid them, but boys can actually make great friends. No, really! Here's why:

Reason one. Got a problem? Talk to a boy — his view on the situation might make you see things differently.

Reason two. Boys are great for adventures, making forts, building tree houses, and inventing obstacle courses.

Reason three. If they are upset with you, boys will often just come right out and tell you what's wrong instead of getting moody or ignoring you.

Reason four. Boys can always be persuaded into doing dares — and can come up with some great ones for you to do, too. (See page 102 to get you started.)

Reason five. Boys are not afraid of getting scraped knees when you're playing a game, which is great for when you want to climb trees or learn to break-dance.

Reason six. If you ask nicely, he might lend you his old skateboard and teach you how to use it. Totally rad!

Reason seven. Boys have the best collections of computer and video games, and often know all the sneakiest cheats and shortcuts to secret levels. Excellent!

Reason eight. They may be able to give you some great tips for wowing your team on the soccer field.

Reason nine. They can give you the insider info on that boy you have a crush on.

True-friend tip. Believe it or not, boys have feelings, too. Make sure you apply the same golden rules of friendship to them as you would to your gal pals (see page 25).

HOW TO TELL IF ONE OF YOUR FRIENDS IS A WEREWOLF

Day to day, werewolves can appear to be completely normal human beings, turning into their wolf form only when there is a full moon. Could one of your friends be leading a double life as a mythical monster? Here are the key signs to look out for.

SIGNS OF THE WOLF

- Her room is covered in what looks like animal hair, but her only pet is a goldfish.

- She will make up weird excuses to stay at home and avoid seeing you whenever there is a full moon, but then

seems very tired the next day for a girl who claims to have had an early night.

- She hates going to the park. Dog whistles play havoc with her ears, even though you can't hear them.

- Her hair and nails grow really, really quickly – she always seems to need a haircut and manicure.

- The day after the full moon, your local paper reports that a strange, hairy being was seen prowling through a nearby field, and prints a blurry picture of the beast. You can't be sure, but you could almost swear the monster was wearing your friend's favorite pink sneakers!

- When she sings along to her favorite pop song, it sounds like howling.

HOW TO PLAY
"THE WINNING SMILE"

Good friends are great to have a giggle with, but sometimes it can be fun when there is no giggling allowed. This game is an excellent way to start a party or to liven up a quiet afternoon.

Stand with your friends in a circle facing each other. Choose one friend to be the Smiler. The rest of you need to keep your faces as straight as possible – no smiling is allowed.

The Smiler must then start to smile the biggest smile she possibly can. Once she is smiling, she must then reach her hand to her face and wipe it across her smile as if she is "taking off" her smile. She must then reveal her smile-free face and "hold" her smile in her fist. She must then "throw" her smile to another player in the circle. This player should then "catch" the smile and put it on her own face. She must then take off her smile and throw it to someone else, as before.

The only rule of this game is that only one player is allowed to smile at any one time. If any of the other players start to grin before they are thrown a smile, they are disqualified and must leave the circle. This game is a lot harder than it sounds!

WINNING SMILES

To make the game extra funny, make a really silly grin whenever it is your turn to be the Smiler. Open your eyes as wide as you can and open your lips to reveal all of your teeth. Or try smiling with your lips clamped shut and smiling only with your cheeks. Experiment with different smiles to see which one gets the most laughs.

HOW TO FORGIVE YOUR FRIEND

You and your friend have had a huge disagreement. She has really hurt your feelings, and even though she has apologized, there is no way that you will ever be able to make up . . . or is there? Discover how you can rescue your friendship before it's too late.

TAKE A LOOK AT THE BIG PICTURE

Step back from the situation and take some time to think about what your friend has done to upset you. Try to think about the "big picture" of your friendship. This means that instead of worrying and getting angry about this hurtful event, look back at all the time you have spent together and consider your friendship as it really is.

Think about why you are friends in the first place — for example, you may have been friends since you were very little, or perhaps you have both been great friends since you moved to a new school. Think of all the good times you have shared together

and ask yourself, "Is this argument worth throwing away our friendship?" The answer is nearly always "No."

BE HONEST WITH YOURSELF

When you know someone better than anyone else does, it means you both know how to hurt each other more than anyone else does. When you are feeling angry about something your friend has said or done, ask yourself if you have ever done anything similar in the past — either to her or to anyone else. It can be really difficult to be this honest with yourself when your feelings have been hurt. But if you are able to admit that you have done some hurtful things in the past, you will find it much easier to forgive your friend.

CLEAR THE AIR

When your friend says she is sorry, let her know exactly why her words or actions hurt you. This way she knows what she is saying sorry for and has a chance to explain herself. Listen to her, then hug and make up.

FORGIVE AND FORGET

There is no point in forgiving your friend if you are going to remind her all the time of what she did. If she has apologized and you have accepted it, try to leave it at that. If you keep on bringing up her mistake, she may get tired of hearing about how much she hurt you and decide to be friends with someone else instead.

True-friend tip. Being a good friend is a decision that you have to make every day. Sometimes this decision is easy, but when you have been hurt, it is much harder. Remember that if both of you still want to be friends, nothing can get in your way.

DARING DEEDS FOR BEST FRIENDS TO DO

Picture the scene: It's a Sunday afternoon, it's raining outside, there's nothing on TV, and you've even rearranged your bedroom out of boredom. Well, be bored no longer. Grab a friend and play a game of dares, and your afternoon will turn into a sidesplitting adventure!

DARING RULES

The rules of daring are very simple. Take turns giving each other tricky tasks to complete. You are allowed two "passes" each. These allow you to get out of doing any dare you don't like. Use them very carefully.

DARING DEEDS

Here are eight dares to get you started, but think of some of your own.

Dare one. Put all your clothes on backward and wear them out to the store.

Dare two. Eat a mouthful of a weird combination of foods — what about smelly cheese and a banana, or cereal with orange juice on it, or cold baked beans with strawberry jam? Yuck!

Dare three. Stand outside the front of your house and sing a really soppy love song at the top of your voice.

Dare four. Run up to the nearest boy and quickly kiss him on the cheek before he knows what hit him.

Dare five. Sing the ABC's while standing on your head.

Dare six. Put your dinner plate on the floor and eat from it like a dog.

Dare seven. Stay silent for the next 15 minutes, even if people speak to you.

Dare eight. Stand in the bathtub or shower and pour an ice-cold cup of water over your head.

True-friend tip. Remember, games are supposed to be fun: Keep things friendly and make sure everyone knows that they don't have to do anything they really don't want to do.

HOW TO MAKE NEW FRIENDS

Whether you have just moved to a new town or simply find it hard to meet fun friends to hang out with, follow these tips and you will soon find it easy to get chatting. You might even get yourself a new best bud.

NEIGHBORHOOD WATCH

Have you seen some other kids playing near your house but have no idea how to start up a conversation? Ask an adult if he or she would mind your going outside near where the other kids are hanging out. Start an activity that you can do alone that might get their attention — for example, roller-skating or bike riding. If they seem interested in what you are doing, why not offer them a turn on your skates or bike? If you smile and act friendly, you're sure to start talking with someone in no time.

GET INVOLVED

Having lots of interests outside of school hours is a fun way of finding and making new friends. Clubs and organizations are great because you will often be put into groups with people and be made to work together. Whatever your interests, you are sure to find a group that reflects them, from basketball to drama to music. You can also ask your parents if you could join your local youth club or Girl Scout troop.

BE APPROACHABLE

If you make yourself look friendly, people will be more likely to want to strike up a conversation with you. Here's how this can be done:

DON'T look at the floor or your shoes. You won't find any new friends there!

DO smile and make eye contact with people.

DO say "Hi." It sounds obvious, but a simple greeting can be enough to get the conversation rolling.

DON'T cross your arms. This makes you look "closed off" and grumpy to others.

DO stand up straight, with your hands in your pockets or by your sides. This will make you look relaxed, confident, and ready for some fun.

DON'T despair. You may not meet them right away, but your new friends are out there and can't wait to get to know you.

HOW TO WRITE A LETTER TO YOUR PEN PAL

You don't have to live in the same town or even country as someone to become friends. With a pen pal, you can get to know someone really well just by writing to them. Today, most people communicate by phone and e-mail, but it's always exciting to receive an envelope in the mail addressed to you.

FIND A PAL

Ask a teacher at school if it is possible for him or her to contact another school somewhere else in the country to see if any of the pupils there would like to start writing to your class. If you are a Girl Scout, why not ask your troop leader to find another troop for you to write to?

There are several groups that help put people in contact with others to write to — often children in foreign countries who are looking for a chance to practice their English. Ask an adult to help you find the details of these organizations online.

PUT PEN TO PAPER

Now that you have your pen pal, what do you write? Staring at a blank sheet of paper can be a bit daunting, so follow these tips to achieve pen pal perfection.

To begin. Take a sheet of writing paper and write today's date in the top right-hand corner. On the left-hand side of your paper write "Dear *your pen pal's name*" and follow this with a comma.

Today's date

Dear XXXX,

Paragraph one. If your pen pal has written to you already, thank her for the letter. Introduce yourself. Tell her your name and your age and where you go to school. You might want to tell her about your family and whether you have any brothers or sisters. End the paragraph with a question – for example, "Do you have any brothers or sisters?"

Paragraph two. Tell your pen pal something interesting that you have done recently – for example, "On Saturday I had some friends over for a sleepover. We had a midnight feast, and it was really fun! What do you like to do on weekends?"

Paragraph three. Tell your pen pal something really cool about your life – for example, "My best friends are named Sara and

Annabel – we call ourselves the Glam Stars and are starting our own band. Who are your best friends?"

Paragraph four. The last paragraph should be a conclusion. Write about how much you are looking forward to hearing back from your pen pal, and ask anything else you would like to know about her life.

Saying good-bye. As this is an informal letter, you can sign off with "Best wishes" or "Yours truly," followed by a comma, then sign your name.

SEND THE LETTER

Before you fold your letter and seal it in an envelope, read over what you've written and make any corrections. Then pop your letter into the envelope.

Write your pen pal's name and address on the front of your envelope and make sure to write your address in the upper left-hand corner of the envelope, in small letters. Stick a stamp in the top right-hand corner and mail your letter. Hopefully, in a few days or weeks, you will be receiving some mail in return!

True-friend tip. If you are writing to somebody who lives in a foreign country, you will need to go to your nearest post office and ask how many stamps you need to put on your letter, because it costs more to send things overseas.

Amy Adams
2 Lark Lane
Sunnydale, CA 98765

Daisy Day
15 Happy Avenue
Middletown, NY 12345
USA

THREE INSTANT BOREDOM BUSTERS FOR YOU AND YOUR FRIENDS

Even the most fun friends can have dull days every now and again. Keep monotonous moments at bay with these quick-and-easy boredom busters.

THE ACCENT GAME

It's good to play the Accent Game in a public place where you will have to speak to lots of other people – for example, in cafés, on buses, or at the mall. Choose a foreign accent that you and your friends are quite confident using. British or Australian accents are good choices, since we are used to hearing them in movies and on TV. Before you start, practice your accent to make sure it sounds realistic. The idea is to pass yourselves off in public as people of a different nationality. Make sure you keep a straight face at all times or the game will be up. Throw in some realistic-sounding detail – for example, if you are in a library, whisper to your friend, "Back home in London, the libraries let you take out only one book at a time. . . ." See how long you can keep it up!

BACKSEAT BINGO

Backseat Bingo is a great way of having fun when you are on a long car ride or on the bus for a school trip. Before you leave, make your bingo cards (see page 110) – one for each friend. Each player needs one of the cards and a pen. When you see or hear one of the items on your card, you should call out that you have it. Once everyone else confirms, you can cross it off your card. The first person to cross off all of the things on her card shouts "Bingo!" and is the winner.

Teacher/parent tells us to "Sssssshhhh!"	A stop sign	A white truck overtakes us on the road.	Someone's cell phone rings.
A horse in a field	An ad on the radio	A café by the roadside	A gas station

THUMB WAR

Thumb War is a two-player game. Stick out your right hands as if you are about to shake hands. Curl your fingers around your friend's fingers and stick your thumbs up in the air. To begin the game, both chant: "One, two, three, four — I declare a thumb war. Five, six, seven, eight — try to keep your thumb straight!" The aim of the game is to pin your friend's thumb underneath your own without unlinking your fingers from hers. Once you have your opponent's thumb held down underneath yours, you say: "One, two, three, four — I have won the thumb war!" You win if you manage to hold her thumb down for the time it takes you to say the rhyme. If you can't, the game's still on!

HOW TO START A GIRL BAND

If you love music, starting a band with your friends can be serious fun! Practicing together and making up songs is a real buzz, and may lead to playing performances in public or entering competitions. You might even set off on the road to superstardom. Here's how to get started.

WHAT TO PLAY

The first thing to think about is what kind of girl band you want to be. Do you imagine yourself and your friends rocking out onstage with guitars and drums? Are you more of a group of pop princesses with a killer sense of style?

ROCK YOUR SOCKS OFF

If you decide on a rocker-chick image for your band, you'll probably want to play your own instruments. Buying your own can get very expensive, so check with your teacher to see if it is possible for you all to join a music group at school where you can use the instruments there for free.

In the meantime, you need to work on your most important instruments – your voices. Practice singing a cappella as much as you can, which means singing together or on your own without any instruments. Singing a cappella will help you to get your voices working together and doesn't cost a penny. Most talent shows ask you to audition a cappella in the first rounds, so get used to it now so that you can wow the judges when the time comes.

DANCING QUEENS

If you want your band to belt out some chart-topping pop hits, then playing musical instruments isn't as important as a series of slick dance moves and some serious singing. Watch lots of music videos for inspiration and decide whether your band will have one lead singer and some awesome backup singers, or whether you will all take turns singing solo.

Try to link your dance moves to the feeling of your song. If it's a fast, exciting song, you could try hip-hop–style moves with lots of energy. If it's a love song, you could all stand in a line and perform small movements, such as snapping the fingers of one hand in time to the rhythm.

Try to imagine performing in front of a big crowd, even when you're just practicing in your bedroom, and incorporate some moves that will get the audience bopping along, such as waving your arms above your head or clapping your hands in time to the beat and encouraging the audience to do the same.

GO YOUR OWN WAY

The most important thing for any girl group is a sense of individuality. Whether you decide to sing songs that you have written yourselves or to belt out your version of a current smash hit, it's really important to add your own style and personality to your songs. Give it that star quality that will make people fall in love with your band.

Think about the different personalities of the members of your band, and try to show them off in the way that each of you dresses and the signature moves that each of you has. For example, if one of your friends is very girly and sweet, her outfit could include a lot of pink, and her signature move could be blowing the audience kisses.

True-friend tip. Get together with your bandmates regularly to brainstorm great new song and dance ideas, and to make sure that each of you is happy with her place in the band.

HOW TO STAY FRIENDS FOR LIFE

Okay, so you're great friends now, but what about in the future? Make sure that you stay best buddies for life by following these top tips.

FOREVER FRIENDS

Promise to be there. Pick a place that is special to you and your friend and promise to meet there at the same time on a specific day (say, 5 P.M. on August 1st) every five years, without fail!

Accept the fact that you will both change. As you grow older, you and your friend will both change and may become quite different from each other. If you accept this change, it can actually make your friendship stronger and more interesting, rather than destroying it.

Be birthday buddies. Always remember each other's birthdays. Buy a special "Birthday Book" to write the dates in, and then you'll have no excuse for forgetting!

Don't let boys come between you. Remember that crushes on boys come and go, but friends are always there.

Remember that newer doesn't mean better. There is an old saying, "Make new friends, but keep the old, for one is silver and the other, gold." Always try to remember this.

Keep smiling. When life gets serious, keep making each other laugh!

Distance doesn't mean doom. If one of you has to move away, see if it is possible to visit her on vacation.

Put pen to paper. Keep in contact by writing and sending each other photos, even if you move thousands of miles away. You can do this by letter and via e-mail. There is no excuse for letting things slide.

True-friend tip. Try to forgive your friend if she sometimes forgets about you. As you get older, and when you have families of your own, life can get busy and friends can temporarily be forgotten. But as long as you make the effort to stay in contact, your friendship will survive.

HOW TO MAKE FRIENDS WITH YOUR PARENTS

Think about it: Only your very best friend knows you better than your parents do. Parents can teach you loads of cool new stuff, and you might find that they give you lots more freedom once you understand each other better. Follow these handy hints to make your folks your friends.

PERFECT PARENT POINTERS

Ask them to teach you something. All grown-ups love to feel that they are experts on something. Here's your chance to learn some cool new skills from your parents, and maybe get a bit closer.

Tell them about your day. Answering questions about your day when you just want to relax can be a real drag. To avoid this, tell your parents a couple of things without being asked, and you'll be free to get on with your evening much sooner. It doesn't have to be anything special – for example, tell them about a new game you played in gym class, or how much you like your new class project.

Find out what makes them tick. After all, they have their own likes, dislikes, and hobbies, just like you. Find out what your dad's favorite music is. You just may discover some cool retro bands that you love as much as he does. If you spend time figuring out what your parents love, you'll learn more about them and you'll get along with them much better.

HOW TO HOLD A SWAP MEET

When your allowance doesn't quite stretch to a shopping spree, a swap meet is a great way to bag yourself some goodies for free. You'll have fun, too. Remember, one person's trash is another's treasure. Here's how:

THREE TO FOUR WEEKS BEFORE

Ask your parents' permission first, then send out invitations to your friends as follows.

You are invited to:

Katie's Swap Meet!

Date: November 11th
Place: Katie's House
Time: 11 A.M.

Please bring a bag or box full of your
unwanted clothes, books, CDs, and anything
else you want to swap.

TWO WEEKS BEFORE

Start assembling your own collection of items to swap. Anything broken or stained is probably not going to be very popular, but clothes you have gotten tired of or grown out of might be perfect for one of your friends. Everyone is a different size and shape and has different tastes, so your castoffs could be their dream outfits! You could also ask any older siblings or friends if they have anything they'd like to donate – they may have outgrown some very cool clothes themselves.

THE DAY BEFORE

Make sure you have a clear space in the house for holding the swap meet. Buy or make any snacks you want to serve for the hungry swappers (see page 32 for one idea).

ON THE DAY

Lay out your own items for swapping on the floor or on a table. When your friends arrive, they can lay out their items, too. Then the swap meet is open!

You can go around the group asking people to introduce their items, and anyone who wants them just shouts out. Alternatively, your swap meet can be like a free yard sale, where everyone wanders about and picks what they like. You can use a downstairs bathroom or the space behind a door as a dressing room if people are bashful about trying clothes on in front of one another.

THE RULES OF THE SWAP

- Only one bagful of stuff to be taken home per person – don't get greedy.

- No secretly reserving stuff before the swap has officially begun.

- Be kind about people's castoffs – the items might not be to your taste, but everyone is different!

- If two people want the same item, the original owner gives it to the person who offers her something she wants to swap with.

True-friend tip. Try on everything you have your eye on — there's no point ending up with even more clothes that don't fit when you've just gotten rid of a batch.

SWAP UNTIL YOU DROP

Hooray! You should now have at least one whole "new" outfit to wear plus other goodies that are "new" to you. There may also be items left over that no one has taken. If so, donate them to your local thrift shop.

READ THEM ALL!

The Boys' Book

The Girls' Book

The Boys' Book
of Survival

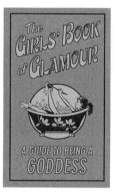

The Girls' Book
of Glamour

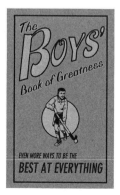

The Boys' Book
of Greatness

The Girls' Book
of Excellence

The Grandmas' Book

The Grandpas' Book

The Dads' Book

The Moms' Book

The Family Book

The Christmas Book

The Girls' Book of Excellence:
Even More Ways to Be the Best at Everything

IF YOU LIKED THIS BOOK, BE SURE TO CHECK OUT:

The Girls' Book of Glamour: A Guide to Being a Goddess

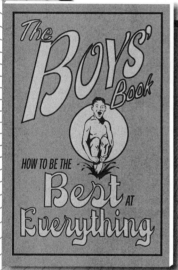
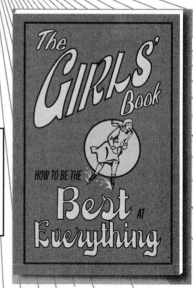

Every parent deserves
THE BEST!

The MOMS' Book

FOR THE MOM WHO'S **Best AT Everything**

- **Host the best parties!**
- **Get the kids to bed at night!**

The DADS' Book

FOR THE DAD WHO'S **Best AT Everything**

- **Be the coolest dad on the block!**
- **Survive with your sanity!**

◣ SCHOLASTIC

www.scholastic.com

MOMDAD

ALSO AVAILABLE:

The Fairy Tale Book

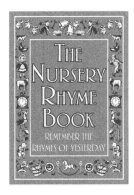

The Nursery Rhyme Book

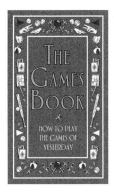

The Games Book

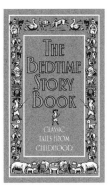

The Bedtime Story Book